Highlights™

시리즈1

창의력 쑥쑥 숨은그림찾기™
Hidden Pictures™

표지 그림 _ 마릴리 해럴드필즈 Marilee Harrald-Pilz

arrow
화살표

sailboat
돛단배

drinking straw
빨대

bird
새

sock
양말

hat
모자

musical note
음표

cane
지팡이

book
책

needle
바늘

ear of corn
옥수수 낱알

tweezers
핀셋

Highlights

slice of pie
파이 조각

candle
양초

fried egg
계란 프라이

drinking glass
유리컵

snail
달팽이

flashlight
손전등

pennant
삼각기

crescent moon
초승달

leaf
나뭇잎

comb
빗

worm
벌레

mushroom
버섯

Illustrated by Paul Richer

handbell
핸드벨

toothbrush
칫솔

spoon
숟가락

coffeepot
커피포트

fishhook
낚싯바늘

key
열쇠

plunger
플런저
(흡인식 하수관 청소기)

heart
하트

mallet
나무망치

pencil
연필

hat
모자

needle
바늘

arrow
화살표

paper clip
클립

envelope
봉투

mug
머그잔

sunglasses
안경

doughnut
도넛

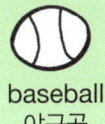
baseball
야구공

banana
바나나

open book
펴놓은 책

A Sticky Situation 끈적끈적해요!

fishhook
낚싯바늘

sailboat
돛단배

toothbrush
칫솔

sock
양말

tack
압정

ladle
국자

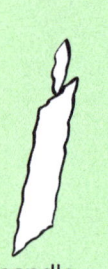
pennant
삼각기

sailboat
돛단배

candle
양초

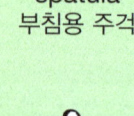
spatula
부침용 주걱

slice of pie
파이 조각

flying disk
비행접시

feather
깃털

button
단추

envelope
봉투

paintbrush
페인트붓

banana
바나나

crescent moon
초승달

toothbrush
칫솔

pencil
연필

Highlights

cat
고양이

nail
못

pennant
삼각기

slice of pie
파이 조각

pencil
연필

key
열쇠

ax
도끼

mug
머그잔

sailboat
돛단배

kite
연

ladder
사다리

spatula
주걱

mallet
나무망치

artist's
brush
그림붓

slice of
bread
빵 조각

needle
바늘

lollipop
막대 사탕

sock
양말

open book
펴놓은 책

Smile! 웃어요!

Koalas and Kangaroos 코알라와 캥거루

handbell
핸드벨

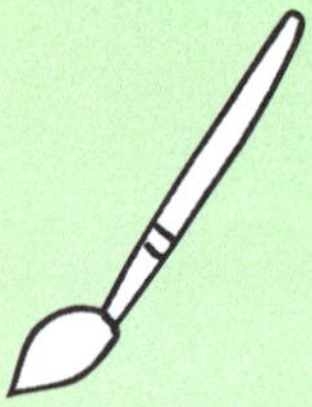

artist's brush
그림붓

ice-cream cone
아이스크림 콘

pencil
연필

glove
장갑

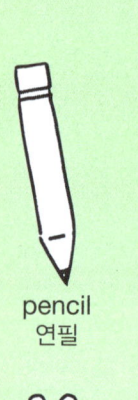

slice of pie
파이 조각

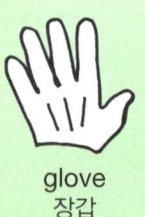

musical note
음표

pitcher
물주전자

hat
모자

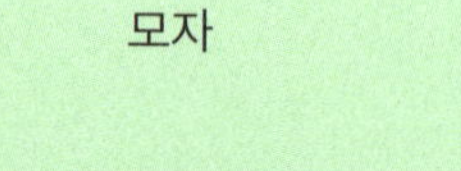

spoon
숟가락

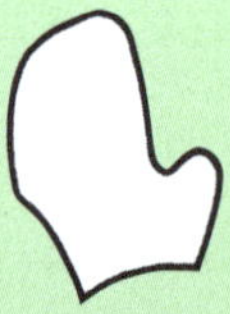

mitten
벙어리장갑

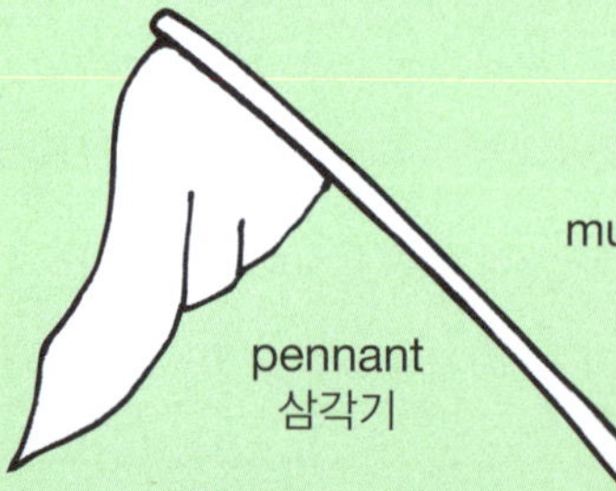

pennant
삼각기

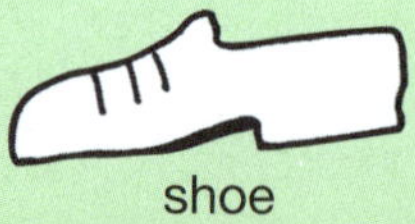

shoe
신발

mushroom
버섯

turtle
거북

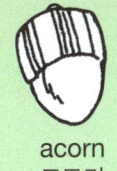

saucepan
냄비

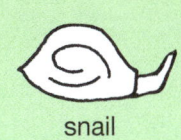

acorn
도토리

snail
달팽이

fish
물고기

banana
바나나

goose
거위

On the Mountain Trail 산길

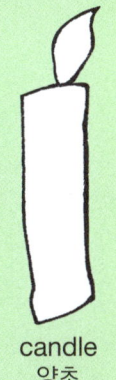

candle
양초

ice-cream bar
막대
아이스크림

bird
새

mitten
벙어리장갑

knitted hat
털모자

ring
반지

Quilting Bee 바느질하는 벌

scissors
가위

closed umbrella
접은 우산

banana
바나나

slice of pizza
피자 조각

number 4
숫자 4

candle
양초

snail
달팽이

safety pin
안전핀

baseball cap
야구 모자

pencil
연필

shark
상어

needle
바늘

rabbit's head
토끼의 머리

frying pan
프라이 팬

tube of
toothpaste
치약튜브

fork
포크

snake
뱀

fishhook
낚싯바늘

slice of pizza
피자 조각

banana
바나나

hammer
망치

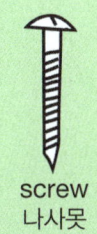
screw
나사못

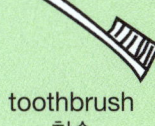
toothbrush
칫솔

heart
하트

pencil
연필

flamingo
플라밍고

Fishing on the Dock 나루터에서 낚시하기

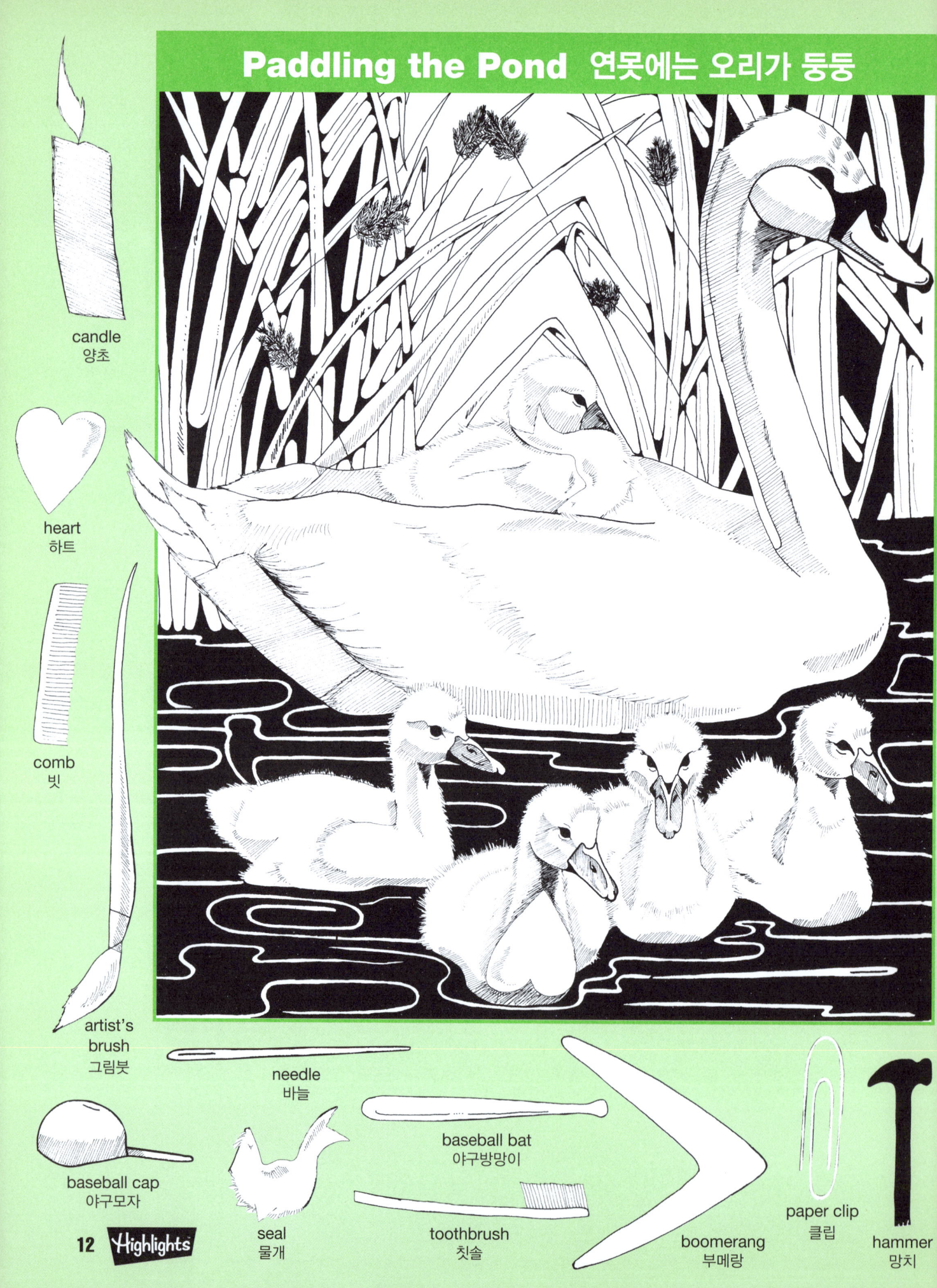

candle
양초

heart
하트

comb
빗

artist's
brush
그림붓

baseball cap
야구모자

seal
물개

needle
바늘

toothbrush
칫솔

baseball bat
야구방망이

boomerang
부메랑

paper clip
클립

hammer
망치

pumpkin
호박

pitcher
물주전자

toothbrush
칫솔

canoe
카누

2 birds
새 두 마리

slice of bread
빵조각

goblet
와인잔

boot
부츠

Campfire Roast 모닥불에 소시지 구워 먹기

heart
하트

teacup
찻잔

ice-cream
cone
아이스크림 콘

candle
양초

golf club
골프채

needle
바늘

sailboat
돛단배

artist's
brush
그림붓

hat
모자

feather
깃털

football
럭비공

heart
하트

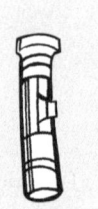

flashlight
손전등

whisk broom
양복솔

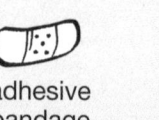

adhesive
bandage
반창고

teakettle
찻주전자

hamburger
햄버거

bell
종

comb
빗

mallet
나무망치

candle
양초

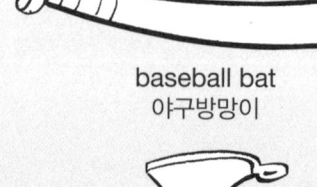

baseball bat
야구방망이

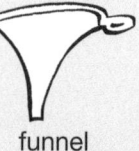

funnel
깔때기

book
책

banana
바나나

sailboat
돛단배

cat mask
고양이 가면

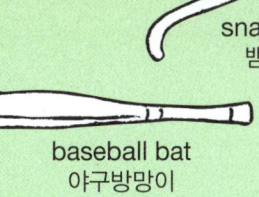
baseball bat
야구방망이

snake
뱀

turtle
거북

Whose Bath? 누구의 목욕?

frog
개구리

bird
새

spoon
숟가락

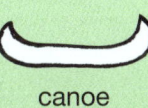
canoe
카누

butterfly
나비

mug
머그잔

fish
물고기

Bookstore Café 생쥐들의 북카페

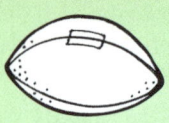
football
럭비공

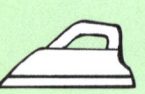
iron
다리미

button
단추

needle
바늘

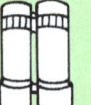
binoculars
쌍안경

envelope
봉투

can
깡통

heart
하트

조용히 하세요!

Highlights

M

flag
깃발

adhesive bandage
반창고

mushroom
버섯

pencil
연필

slice of bread
빵조각

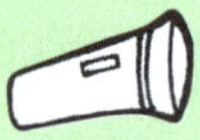

banana
바나나

flashlight
손전등

comb
빗

16  Highlights

worm
벌레

hairbrush
머리빗

party hat
파티 모자

candle
양초

bird
새

thimble
골무

bean
강낭콩

sailboat
돛단배

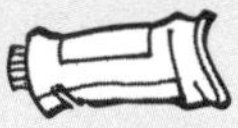

Illustrated by Susan Dahlman

tube of
toothpaste
치약튜브

bell
종

bowl
그릇

lemon
레몬

canoe
카누

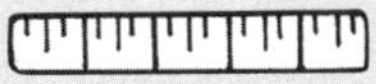

ruler
자

spool of thread
실패

Jungle Family 밀림 가족

eyeglasses
안경

seal
물개

banana
바나나

fork
포크

duck
오리

candle
양초

fish
물고기

whale
고래

penguin
펭귄

goose
거위

dog
개

feather
깃털

Highlights

star
별

feather
깃털

fish
물고기

fishhook
낚싯바늘

funnel
깔때기

muffin
머핀

comb
빗

ruler
자

pointy hat
뽀족 모자

Snow-asaurus 눈으로 만든 공룡

crescent moon
초승달

ghost
유령

teacup
찻잔

seashell
조개껍질

sock
양말

heart
하트

candle
양초

Croc Croquet 악어들의 크로케 경기

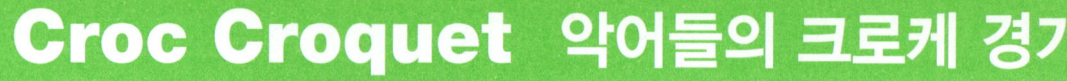

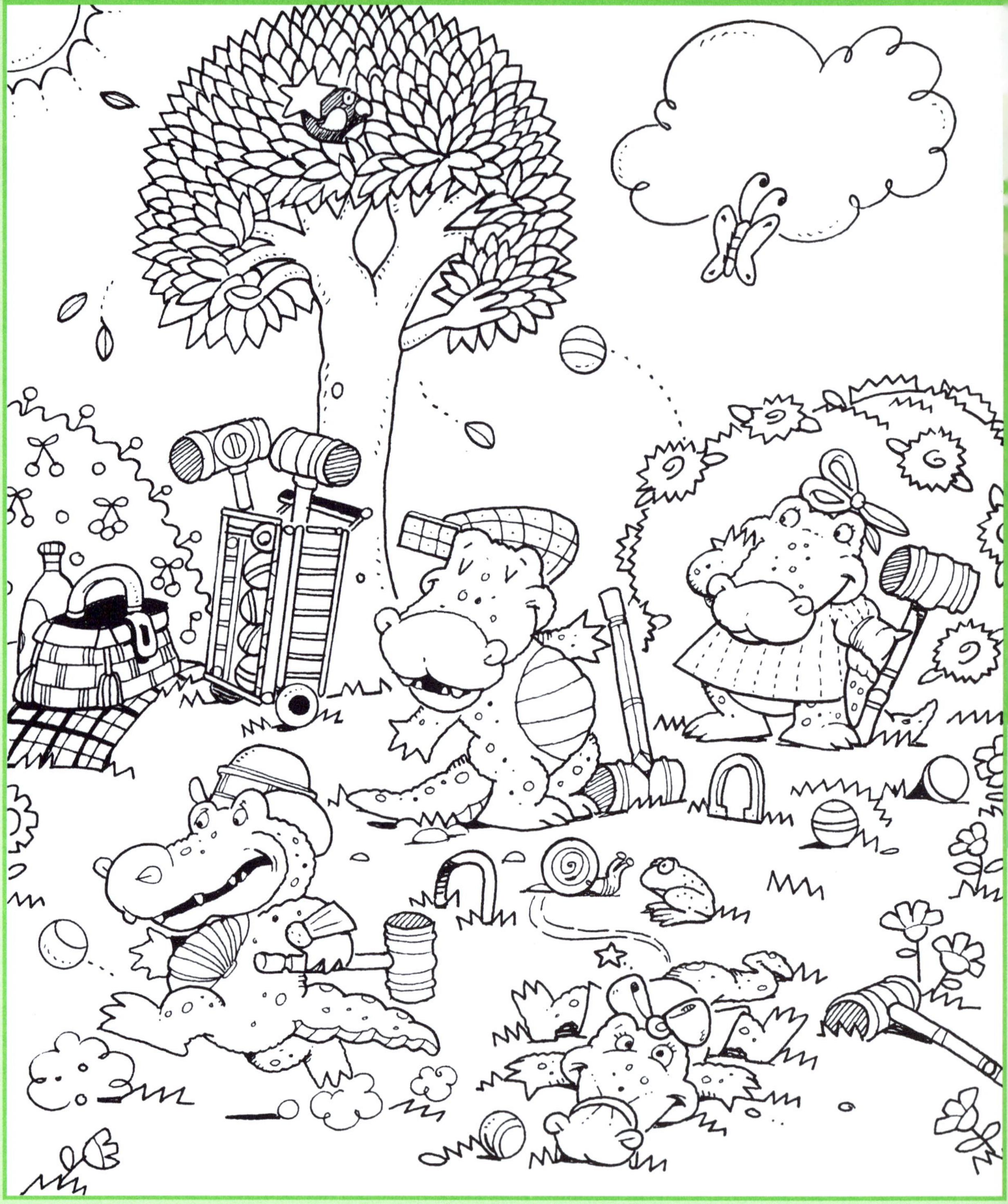

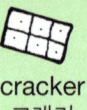

cracker
크래커

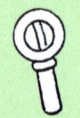

magnifying glass
돋보기

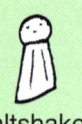

saltshaker
소금 뿌리개

scissors
가위

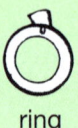

ring
반지

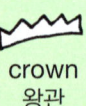

crown
왕관

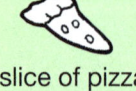

slice of pizza
피자 조각

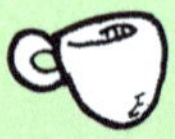

teacup
찻잔

horseshoe
편자
(말발굽에 붙이는 쇳조각)

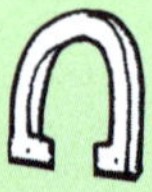

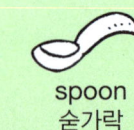

spoon
숟가락

star
별

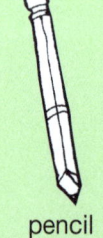

pencil
연필

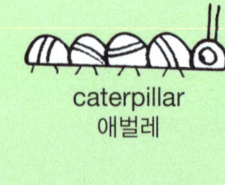

caterpillar
애벌레

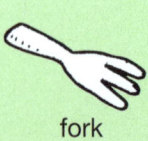

fork
포크

tack
압정

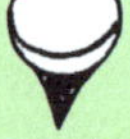

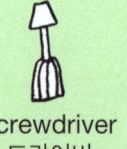

screwdriver
드라이버

bowl
그릇

seashell
조개껍질

ladder
사다리

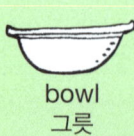

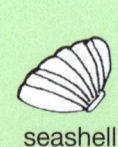

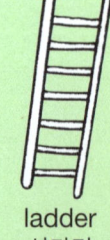

nail
못

mushroom
버섯

heart
하트

toothbrush
칫솔

crescent moon
초승달

ring
반지

pretzel
프레첼
(매듭 모양의 과자)

banana
바나나

spoon
숟가락

star
별

pencil
연필

candle
양초

fork
포크

needle
바늘

sock
양말

Fun on the Dock 나루터 물놀이

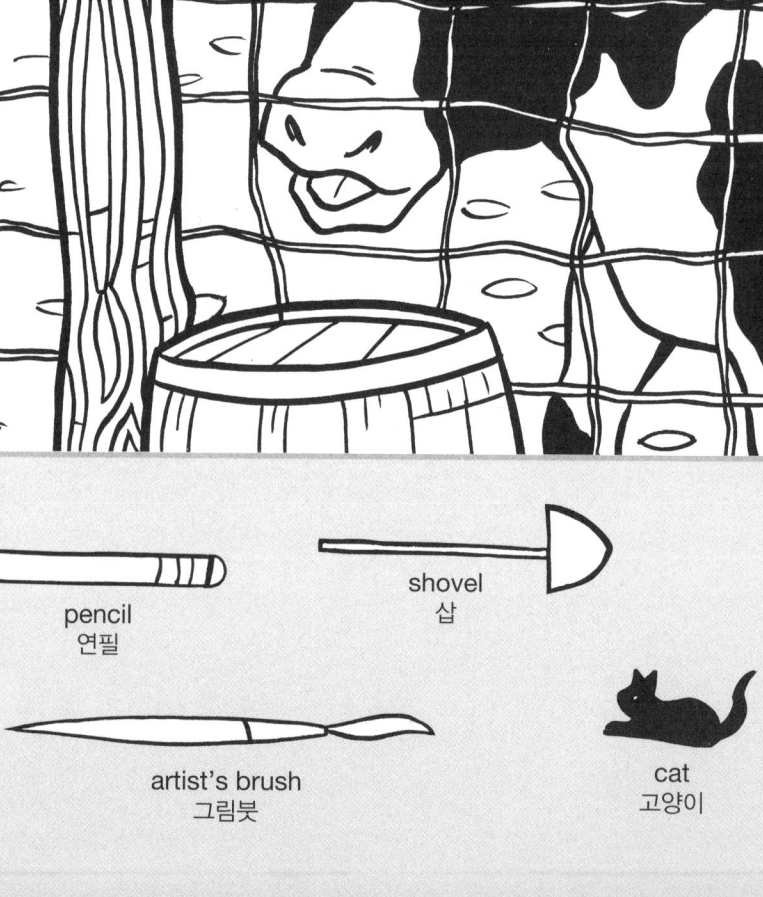

toothbrush
칫솔

sock
양말

slice of pie
파이 조각

tweezers
핀셋

bowling pin
볼링 핀

heart
하트

paper clip
클립

duck
오리

sailboat
돛단배

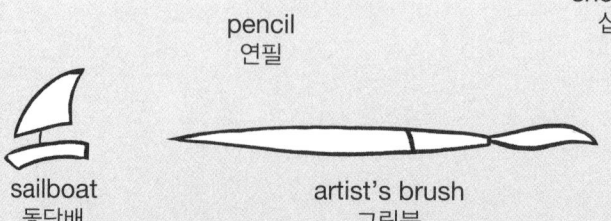

pencil
연필

shovel
삽

artist's brush
그림붓

cat
고양이

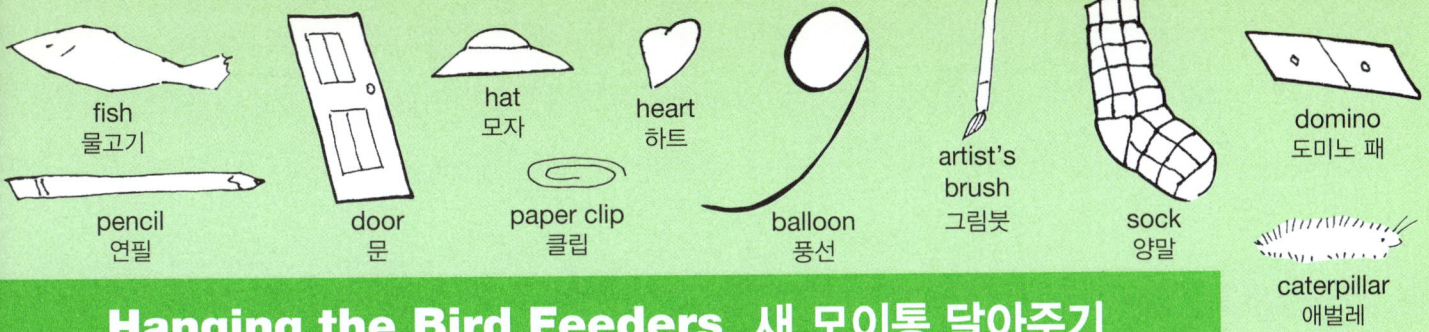

fish
물고기

pencil
연필

door
문

hat
모자

paper clip
클립

heart
하트

balloon
풍선

artist's
brush
그림붓

sock
양말

domino
도미노 패

Hanging the Bird Feeders 새 모이통 달아주기

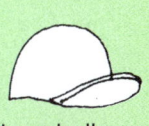
caterpillar
애벌레

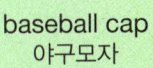
baseball cap
야구모자

candy kiss
사탕

candle
양초

flashlight
손전등

sailboat
돛단배

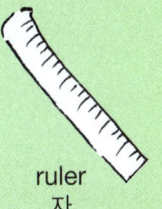
ruler
자

book
책

lollipop
막대 사탕

carrot
당근

pear
배

ice-cream
cone
아이스크림 콘

toothbrush
칫솔

baseball cap
야구모자

bat
박쥐

fish
물고기

slice of cake
케이크 조각

worm
벌레

open book
펴놓은 책

needle
바늘

hippopotamus
하마

telephone receiver
전화 수화기

hammer
망치

pitcher
물주전자

rabbit
토끼

hat
모자

boot
부츠

spatula
주걱

ring
반지

knitted hat
털모자

ice-cream cone
아이스크림 콘

Cookie Fun with Grandpa 할아버지와 쿠키 만들기

bell
종

ladder
사다리

candle
양초

canoe
카누

cat
고양이

shoe
신발

golf club
골프채

broom
빗자루

Ready to Run 달릴 준비

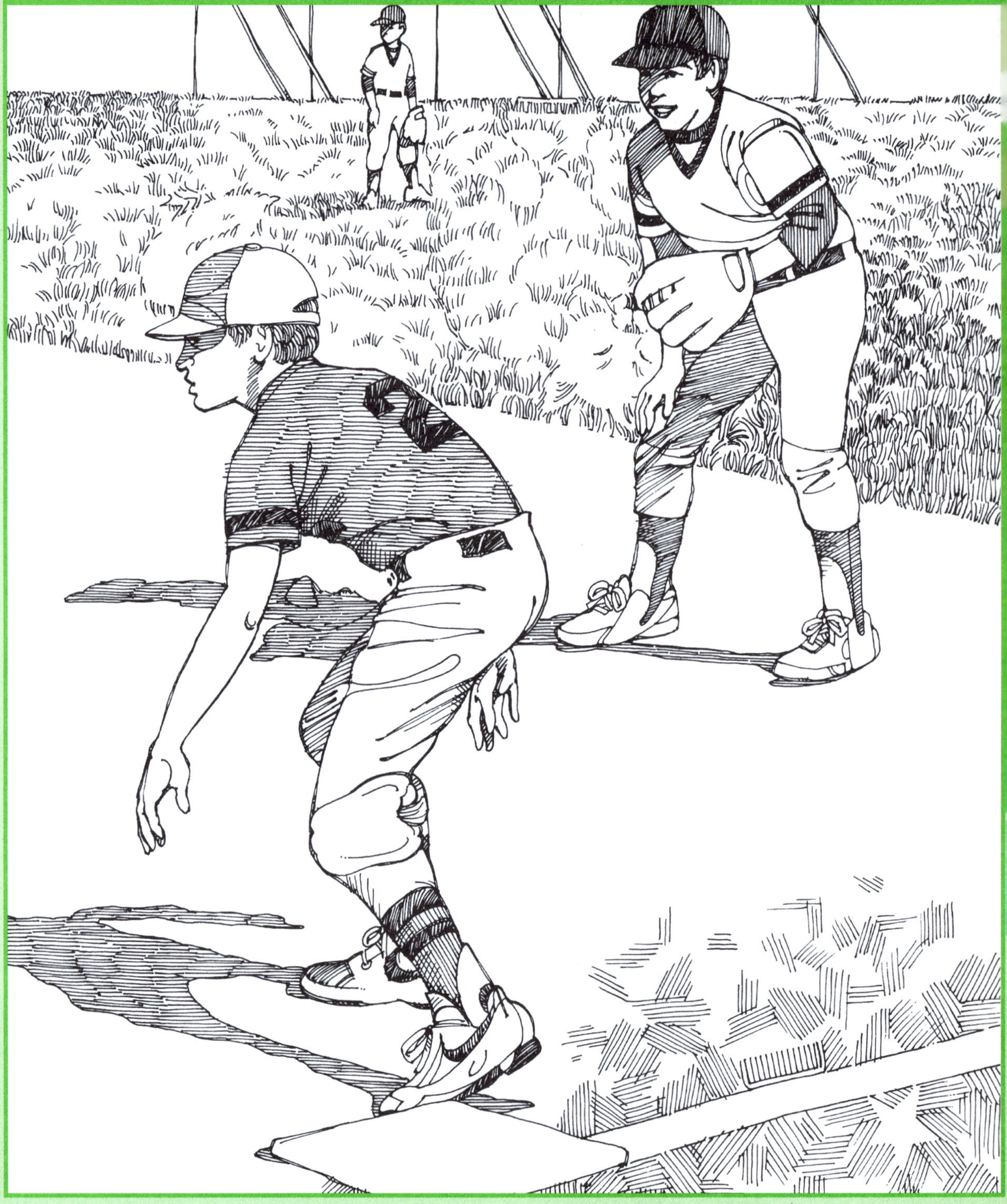

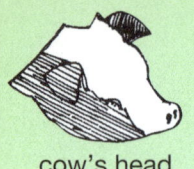

cow's head
젖소의 머리

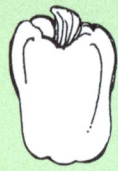

pepper
피망

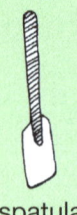

spatula
주걱

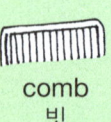

comb
빗

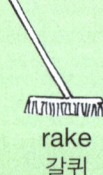

rake
갈퀴

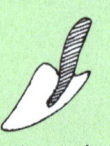

trowel
꽃삽

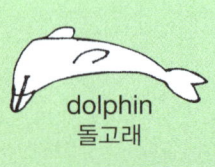

dolphin
돌고래

fork
포크

duck
오리

mug
머그잔

star
별

cat
고양이

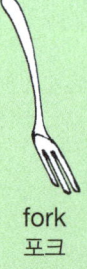

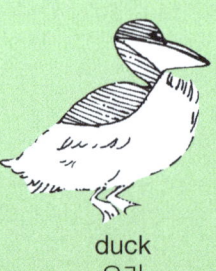

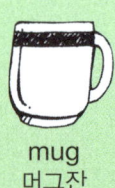

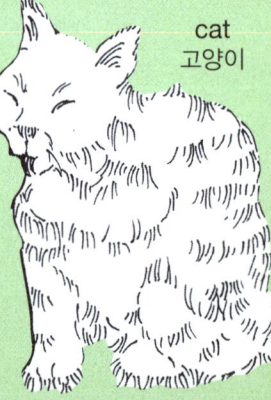

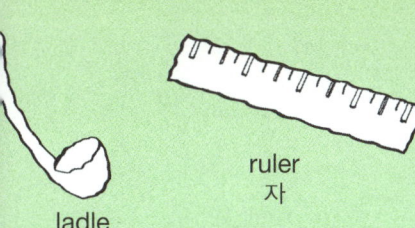

ladle
국자

ruler
자

ice-cream cone
아이스크림 콘

button
단추

envelope
봉투

teacup
찻잔

Paving the Street 도로 포장

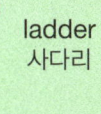

ladder
사다리

sponge
스펀지

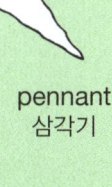

pennant
삼각기

comb
빗

nail
못

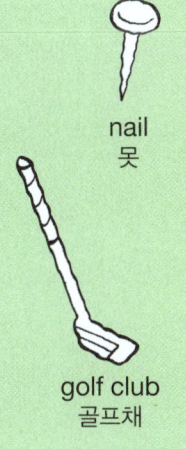

golf club
골프채

slice of pie
파이 조각

ring 반지

banana 바나나

ladder 사다리

star 별

comb 빗

dinosaur 공룡

heart 하트

glove 장갑

boomerang 부메랑

kite 연

party horn 파티 나팔

frog 개구리

eagle's head 독수리의 머리

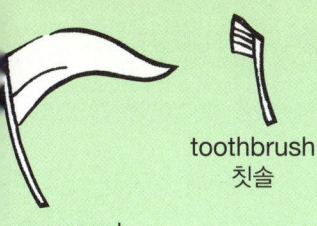
pennant
삼각기

toothbrush
칫솔

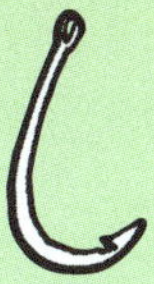

fishhook
낚싯바늘

bird
새

ring
반지

snow cone
스노 콘

mug
머그잔

bell
종

lollipop
막대사탕

The Piñata 신나는 피냐타 파티

fish
물고기

closed
umbrella
접은 우산

boomerang
부메랑

funnel
깔때기

top hat
남성 정장용 모자

mouse
쥐

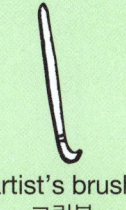
artist's brush
그림붓

slice of pizza
피자 조각

ice-cream
cone
아이스크림 콘

hammer
망치

heart
하트

golf club
골프채

shovel
삽

mushroom
버섯

safety pin
안전핀

ladle
국자

paper clip
클립

pretzel
프레첼
(매듭 모양의 과자)

bird
새

button
단추

comb
빗

Highlights

fork
포크

envelope
봉투

pencil
연필

banana
바나나

ring
반지

spoon
숟가락

Illustrated by Arieh Zeltich

2 keys
열쇠 두 개

hand mirror
손거울

crescent moon
초승달

sock
양말

coat hanger
옷걸이

clothespin
빨래집게

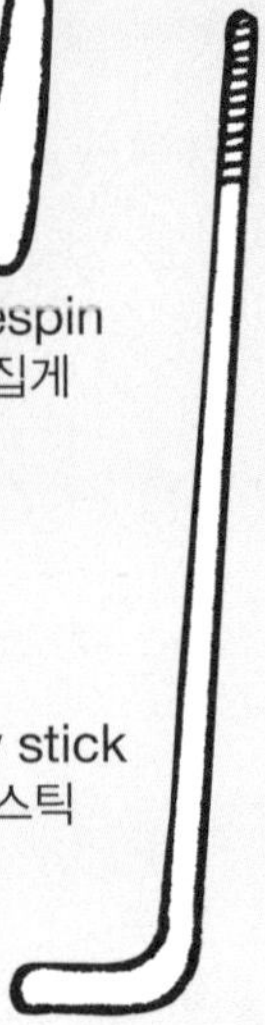

hockey stick
하키 스틱

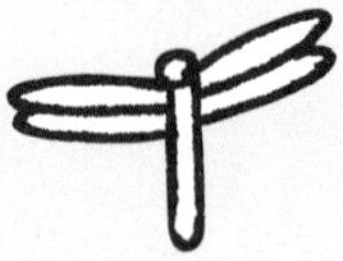

dragonfly
잠자리

glove
장갑

drinking
straw
빨대

crescent
moon
초승달

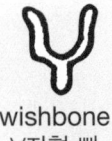

wishbone
V자형 뼈

crown
왕관

magnet
자석

hammer
망치

domino
도미노 패

candle
양초

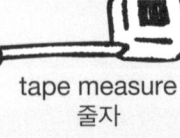

tape measure
줄자

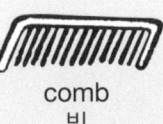

comb
빗

Highlights

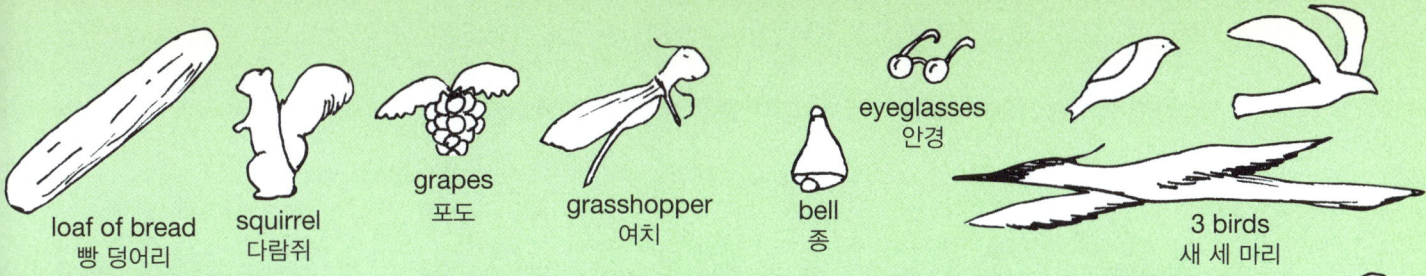

loaf of bread
빵 덩어리
squirrel
다람쥐
grapes
포도
grasshopper
여치
bell
종
eyeglasses
안경
3 birds
새 세 마리

Family Outing 가족 나들이

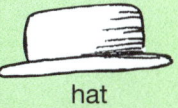

goose
거위
hat
모자
tepee
천막집
candle
양초
fish
물고기
dog's head
개의 머리
celery
셀러리

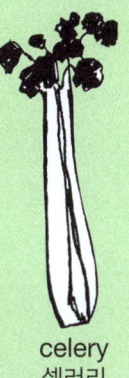

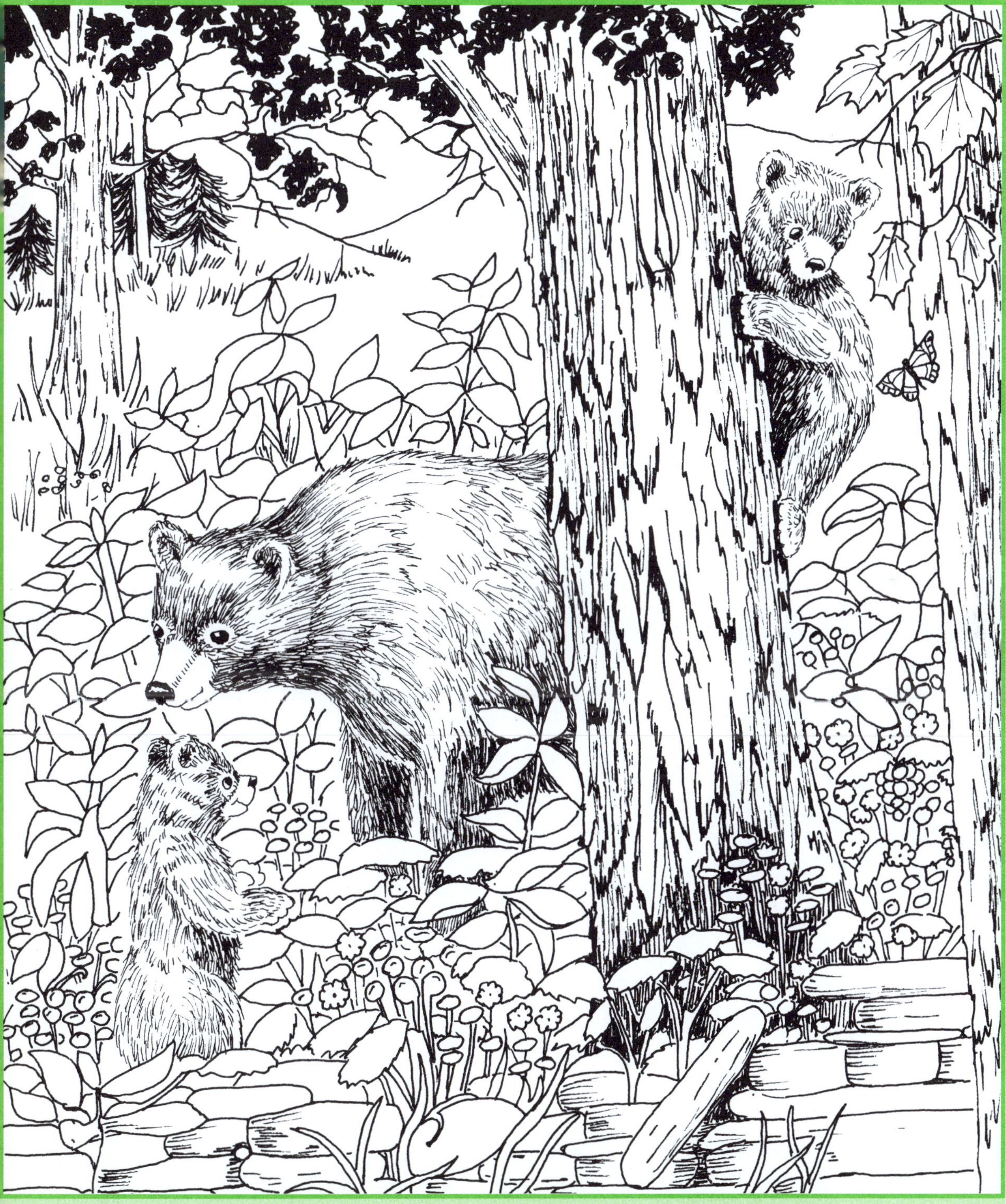

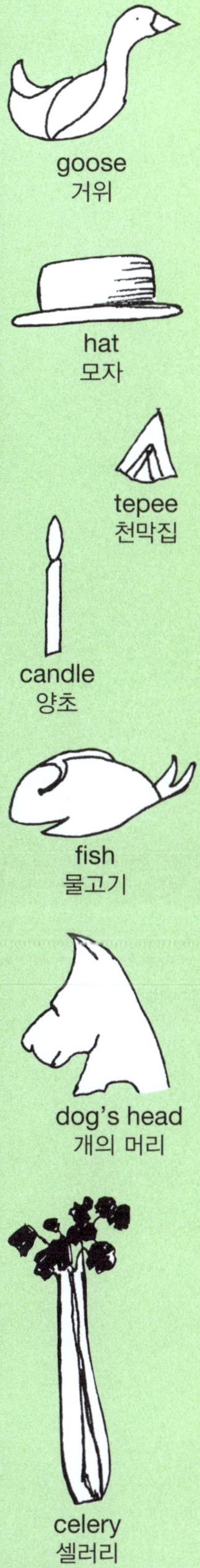

Card Game 카드 게임

tack
압정

mitten
벙어리장갑

heart
하트

ring
반지

pennant
삼각기

candle
양초

comb
빗

ice-cream bar
막대
아이스크림

hatchet
손도끼

crescent
moon
초승달

egg
계란

bird
새

fish
물고기

open book
펴놓은 책

bell
종

mug
머그잔

pointy hat
뽀족 모자

doughnut
도넛

Highlights

tack
압정

drinking glass
유리컵

needle
바늘

telescope
망원경

lollipop
막대사탕

pear
배

ladder
사다리

flashlight
손전등

High Jump 더 높이 높이!

golf club
골프채

trowel
꽃삽

slice of pie
파이 조각

ring
반지

ski
스키

sailboat
돛단배

teacup
찻잔

drinking glass
유리컵

artist's brush
그림붓

slice of pie
파이 조각

horse
말

swan
백조

arrow
화살표

sailboat
돛단배

frog
개구리

shoe
신발

crescent moon
초승달

clothespin
빨래집게

mushroom
버섯

pencil
연필

tulip
튤립

whale
고래

saw
톱

cat
고양이

crescent moon
초승달

cupcake
컵 케이크

toothbrush
칫솔

glove
장갑

button
단추

needle
바늘

banana
바나나

Spring Day 화창한 봄날

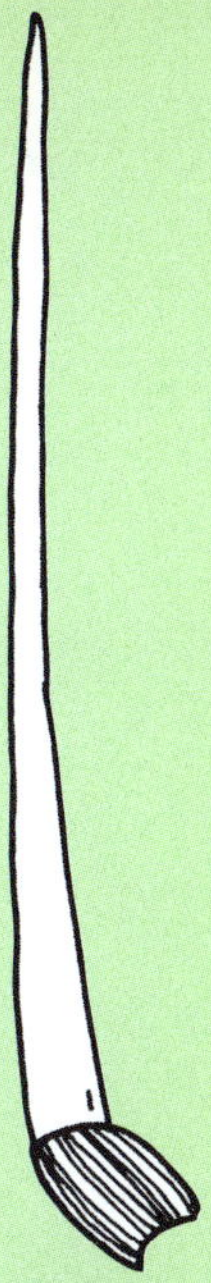

artist's
brush
그림붓

sock
양말

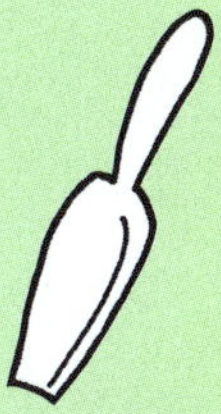

trowel
꽃삽

football
럭비공

mushroom
버섯

sunglasses
선글라스

rabbit
토끼

A Friendly Visit 다정한 방문

snake
뱀

ring
반지

hatchet
손도끼

rabbit
토끼

jar
병

key
열쇠

butterfly
나비

sock
양말

shoe
신발

sailboat
돛단배

bird
새

pennant
삼각기

paintbrush
페인트붓

teacup
찻잔

toothbrush
칫솔

needle
바늘

fish
물고기

slice of pie
파이 조각

fishhook
낚싯바늘

scissors
가위

trowel
꽃삽

shovel
삽

pencil
연필

teacup
찻잔

cupcake
컵케이크

tweezers
핀셋

crescent
moon
초승달

heart
하트

worm
벌레

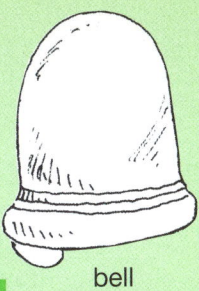

bell
종

Feeling Better? 괜찮아졌니?

빨리
나으세요!

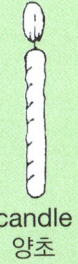

candle
양초

apple
사과

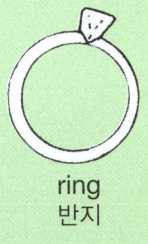

ring
반지

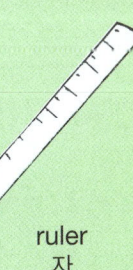

ruler
자

baseball
야구공

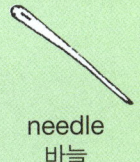

needle
바늘

▼2~3페이지

▼4페이지

▼5페이지

▼6페이지

▼7페이지

▼8페이지

▼9페이지

정답

▼10페이지

▼11페이지

▼12페이지

▼13페이지

▼14페이지

▼15페이지

▼16～17페이지

조용히 하세요!

▼18페이지

▼19페이지

▼20페이지

▼21페이지

▼22페이지

▼23페이지

▼24페이지

▼25페이지

정답

▼26페이지

▼27페이지

▼28페이지

▼29페이지

▼30~31페이지

▼32페이지

▼33페이지

▼34페이지

▼35페이지

▼36페이지

▼37페이지